NECTAR

THE COMPLETE TWO-PART POETRY COLLECTION

NEIL J. FOX

This book is a big warm thank you.

A thank you for supporting me in pouring my passion into what has become this project of self-fulfillment through writing personal and honest poetry.

A thank you for openly willing to listen, read, relate, understand, and interpret my words printed onto the page as something greater.

A thank you to those who inform me that my ambition has inspired you towards reigniting your own individual passions, now looking to set them ablaze.

Cheers to you, and cheers to us.

NECTAR

I

DREAMLAND, SOMEWHERE ELSE

'There is nothing noble in being superior to your fellow man; true nobility is being superior to your former self.'

— Ernest Hemingway

PART 1

A HERO'S JOURNEY

1

entrance to the underworld

AVERAGE JOE

There he goes, yes that's him
Alas, just another average Joe

A boy of simple recognition
No talent, acclaim or anything to show

Kudos aplenty, or a lack thereof
Just another guy lacking his godly glow

Easily forgotten as he fits to the mould
Level of talents recognised an all-time low

Content with life but only on the surface
The exterior facade his weakest of woe

Considered normal, whatever that is
A lack of substance from head to toe

Alone in the world or so he thinks
Longing daily for his very own beau

This specific individual you may not meet
But are more alike than you could possibly know

LOVES ME, LOVES ME NOT

A flick of a petal, swallowing my pride
Deep in my soul the butterflies fly
Flustered, I take another breath

LOVES ME

A steady drive down the lane of despair
Crossing the hazy highway, I proceed with caution
Hairs on my neck stand stiff

LOVES ME NOT

I look to the sky in search of hope
Not a man of faith, but a believer in fate
Through the wild blue yonder, the cosmos are clear

LOVES ME

A realist approach to a surreal situation
Hope for the best, prepare for the worst
As a self-proclaimed realist, I admit my unreadiness

LOVES ME NOT

CRACKHEAD

Higher than high
Craving your presence
Just a touch

No cause for concern
Looking for my next bump
Ready to make the jump

A non-negotiable deal
Light of my life
Colours other than blue

A natural state of euphoria
The source of my pain
Simultaneously my saviour

Adamantine addiction
A release of endorphins
Sick to my stomach

AUTHENTICITY

A dip of my toe into the known unknown
Creeping from the shadows, taking a mere peak

It comes to you over time, a cliché some might say
Sadly, as some never allow it to settle at all

Along the already rocky road you encounter disguised enemies
Attempting to drown you before you know how to swim

Burdened of your fabricated reputation
But instead allowing yourself to just be

Time and awareness become close companions
Enabling you to eventually swing the door open with force

If considered a witch, then burn me at the stake
As flames of my unapologetic authenticity will exhilarate

To both age and the senses, I hang up my coat
Swarmed in the midst of revelation

A TALE OF TWO BOYS

Two hearts
One undeniable connection of chemistry
And an indestructible force that nothing can halt
This is the tale of two boys

A hate crime to the heteronormative
The sweet seduction of a second-class classification
Misunderstanding of a simple preference
As if a life-threatening condition

Hand holding in public
Indulging in the idea of a white picket fence
Simply existing in a world that we created
Happy together

A longing hope to be ignored
Wondering if heads will never not turn
A desire for a day that there will never need be
A tale of two boys

MAN OF STEEL

A curse of kryptonite
What doesn't kill you makes you stronger
Still alive and growing powerless, on the contrary
A sucker punch to the soul, I'm losing strength

Merely mortal
A vessel of my being
Becoming deprived of my superpower to survive
Is anybody still inside?

Survival instinct
Through consistency of uncertainty
Considered a lover, with no alternative but to fight
Thickening of my skin as I turn to stone

As warmth leaves my body, I climatize
In my defence I have no control
I am not the chosen one as I needed saving
And sadly, I become a man of steel

THE UNIVERSE

Riding the rings of Saturn
Existence through the Creation of Adam
Gravitational attraction binding the stars and dark matter
As time is the most powerful force of all

The most beautiful being we cannot touch
As our insignificance highlighted through our limitations
Deep seeded emotions and feelings are always valid
All in all, we still matter

We must learn to travel not only through time
Through space, humanity, mentality and understanding
For our existence is but a speck of dust
On the unopened wardrobe of opportunity

Enlightenment of a larger kind
Like the 10 billion light years lighting the abyss
We must all find our incredible and our beautiful
And let it shine through the darkest of times

SERENDIPITY

Plunging through the depths of my deepest desires
Educating myself an earnest student

A cliché is a cliché for a reason
We need to learn to identify the source in stride

Familiar paths we can walk in the dark
And the shortcuts we create with the intent to survive

The only beliefs and opinions valued our own
In the knowing decisions made hell-bent for good

Surrounded by peers, acquaintances and strangers a plenty
And I'm going to enter talking

What was once my vice, is now my virtue
My superpowers the serendipity of my awakened soul

I take a seat in the winter of my coming of age
Going, going, gone -

METAMORPHOSIS: THE MINEFIELD HARVEST

I catch myself caught in revelations
When the mines of the minefield blow
Blasting away the surface land
Left mind blown

Of transformations, that often unknowingly occur
As simple as from rain to snow, even bread to toast,
And as every great Alchemist knows
Like that of even lead to gold

The hero embarking on his never-ending journey
Challenges encountered along the way
A story moving at unprecedented pace
With the varying characters rotatingly faced

Cocooning now, I think at least
About the racecourses I once ran
Even the times that I had fallen
But countlessly getting back up to stand

Through forced consciousness
I absorb the powers of the past
Learning lessons from mistakes made
Cause baby, I was born to last!

So now I seek to source the fruits
Of my labour among this landmine
Fresh from the forest of righteousness
Harvested metamorphosis

And I believe I may have found it.

2

from california,
with love

POOLSIDE

A bigger splash
Dive so deep I'm over my head
Kaleidoscope of blue
A fresh feeling of new beginning

The glistening chill of liberation
A fantasy
Some said would never come true
Part of the new classic

Flirting with success
Another concoction of juice
Feeling in the atmosphere
Anything is possible

A sense of sustainability
Reassurance to be rest assured
Floating above the surface
Holding my breath

BABY PINK BONNET

Let's arise and go now
To where the sun shines bright in Nevada
90 miles per hour
The wind is strong
On the baby pink bonnet

Laughing hard and singing soft
My skin is hot
My feet not at all cool
The sun is soaring and watching
Over that baby pink bonnet

A look of reassurance
Glistening shades and a cracking smile
The indescribable feeling in my core
There's nowhere I would rather be
Behind this baby pink bonnet

The sun has set, or yet to rise
Gazing up at the night sky through double glazed glass
Dreaming, wishing and maybe hoping
For always night and day
Someday
Of that baby pink bonnet

CITY STAR

Top of the world we're sipping red wine
A dream I never knew
Side by side we're together
Tomorrow I'm giving up, but not tonight

Glamorously gleaming and glistening
A dream come true
I understand, I'm not a fool
But I can feel the love tonight

A melting clock in Hollywood
Dali and Hockney combined
Window gazer, city escaper
Learning and dreaming at once
This whole new fantastic point of view
Is already coming to an end of its time

This city is crazy
And so am I, about you
Overlooking city stars in the city of stars
With you, a city star

BEVERLY HILLS

Dreamy
Tall and beautiful
Shining bright
Beverly Hills

So pretty
Got it all
So they say
Beverly Hills

Enticing
Half full or empty
Anything at all
Beverly Hills

A good game spoken
Facade to be believed
Not anymore
Beverly Hills

THE TASTE OF CHAMPAGNE

Moet Moet
Welcome to the Good Life
My inner desires electrified
Is this the taste of champagne?

We may never be royals
Golden elixir lines our throats
Not a celebration in sight
I love the taste of champagne

A victorious lap of luxury
We toast again, and again
Will it ever get tiresome?
The taste of champagne

Moet Moet
Crystal ball to the unforeseeable
Thirst quenched; taste buds teased
I've a thirst for more champagne

IN CASABLANCA

Timeless classic retold
Emotion translates through era
Another time, place and soul
Something I've felt before

In Casablanca

Yet something significant is bubbling
A coincidence too coincidental
Nor do I believe in the Universe
I'm second guessing myself now

In Casablanca

Have a yen for Utopia
The crashing shores of Malibu
Or a stretch of streets through Dublin
Can reminisce time and time again
Of a crowded gin joint

In Casablanca

JUST A FAN

Idolised lover
And a not-so-secret admirer
Artistic substance treasured
Collaborating feat on the horizon

A double-edged sword
Die-hard obsessed brainstorming for more
I suppress moments of anticipated bliss
Moves made calculated and adored

I never believed the city was haunted
Billboards modest, carpets faded
Hollywood Forever
A California summer never seemed so cold

An iron anchor for a heart
The coast clear, and dreary some
Memories inked like an autograph
As I'm reminded once more of my role

DREAMLAND, SOMEWHERE ELSE

A window gaze embracing mindful desertion
Beige walls, a capsule filled with blue

Surrounded by belongings, lacking the sense
Not here but there, anywhere

The blanket of night darkens the street
Illuminates the manifestation of imagination

A yearning for escape, complete desperation
The pleading prisoner craving release

An unattainable dream now a regular reality
The clock spills wisdom, reflective of time

Desired destinations hold no coordinates
An inbound voyage greets a warm welcome

A dreamland, somewhere else

THE BILLBOARDS

Standing steady, arms folded
Hovering over the swamp below
I am standing atop the balcony
The stars still hold a fairly faded glow

As the city stays on a winding loop
The wolves of the wild howl
Sinners still very much at sin
My own body in pensive prowl

Now eye-level to the billboards
They have always tried to tell me how to think
Directing me towards what they know best
Showcased with their lustreless ink

But the paper has become far too thin
I can clearly see the quality of the print
Although the message was always present
I never really had to squint

I didn't fall for any advertised fantasy
Never, was I going to be led askew
The time and date of which you had me
I was only passing through

Because they don't know what I know
And I now know how they're made
I know how long nothing lasts,
And just how quick that things can change

The world beneath will keep moving
But I will always be the same
Today it's something and tomorrow another
I've finally figured out the rules to the game

A billboard stays sitting still
Erected over the madness ensuing beneath
Throughout the hysteria of time
I master my calmness to an almighty increase

Eye-level on the other side
Of the looking glass, and looking back
I can see with a flipped perspective
I myself, was the only sign I ever lacked

Because I have opened pandora's box
Now I hold the lock and key
I can read between the billboard's lines
A vision of my own future, I can foresee

Tonight atop the balcony, I bow my head
Having learnt which is what to comprehend
With peaceful gratitude I can tell
The billboards in which the corners bend

3

speculation

INTO MY OWN

A phoenix rising from the ashes,
Happened before and to come again,
Fall seven times, stand up eight

Memorable, but not so familiar
A place I've been before
Souvenirs and postcards not requested

The script word for word
I try to catch myself but I'm out of control
Speculation of a right move, I'll never know

Self-actualisation of an ever-changing man
Bullseye to a moving target
I aim, I aim again

The most qualified for the role
Needlessly reminded
This is what you came for

The curtains calling another time
This time I'm coming
Into my own

THE GREATER GAMBLE

All dressed up, ready to go
Yet things are moving slower than slow
A speedy start at a hesitating halt
Time and time, again
Push has come to shove
The dice rotates in a clenched hand
Sweating
The playing board and aspirations simultaneous
They are in clear sight
Pensive pondering of how simple it seems
How do so many others get by?
What seems like a headache puzzle
A walk in the park for others
Risking it all
The cards are dealt
I'm confident in my hand
I've got this one in the bag
Then as suspected
Gameplay alters the outcome
He couldn't read my poker face
Or so I thought
Suspecting more players entered the game
A full house
The game now playing in my mind
I fold again

BITE THE DUST

10:41pm in London
Splash of emotion on a white linen canvas
Muffled TV sounds, echoes of cosmopolitan
Another one bites the dust

The protagonist has fallen
A round of applause for a great effort
An encore, a new cast will form
Another one bites the dust

Growing tiresome but I carry on
Previously ignored red flags wave strong
This time my prerogative
I'm going to bite the dust

Life imitates art
The Taking of Christ
Out of the doorway the bullets rip
Another one bites the dust

A cause for concern
A fixed target or running joke
And another one
You know how this ends

Aspire
to inspire
others
and the
universe
will take
note.

SAFE SPACE

And I think of it
My little light up red runners
Making my mark on the planet
From the word go
Creating

Attempting to eliminate myself
Of subconscious conditioning from birth
Questioning everything
The bigger picture
The smaller print

Why two? Why three?
And even still, why me?
The thoughts that gather
In the magnificent wasteland
Of my safe space

Peace on earth
And I can't wait for heaven

STRANGER FACES

I see your face
in strangers faces
Familiarity in unfamiliar forms
Adaption of the highest form

The darkest place
Is yet the most comforting
I live in my head
Wondering what's happening in yours

End of the world
Are you growing tired of my love?
By the way (I still love you)
Oh, lonesome me

Chiaroscuro
My riches are poorly
In strangers faces
I see your face

DIADEM

Through animality and impurity
And confusion of thought, a man descends

A stroke of genius
A fitting ahead of my coronation of absolution

For our problems will be a freckle upon the foot of the Universe
A fraction to the ultimate ego

Achievement my crown of effort
The diadem of my thoughts

An outstanding revolution
A case of evolution for the mind of man

A coming of age we don't all come to see
In the end, our no longer phased beings will be set free

With self-control and resolution,
And considered thought, a man ascends

(FOR)EVER ENOUGH

Come see about me
Sitting here wondering what we were ever going to be
Lurking only leads to being let down
Speculation of your selfish actions
A simple act of self-sabotage

Ever enough, will I ever be?
Forever enough for a stranger to come

A longing for a solution
The equations and the sums all add up
Lying awake at night still trying to solve it all
Restarting over for a resolution
Right again, wrong answer

Ever enough, will I ever be?
Forever enough for a stranger to come

Playing a fool
Wondering my worth
You say one thing and mean another
Acting a messer and I'm the jester?
Here I stay riding the waves of wonder

ELIXIR

A recent discovery
Of true celestiality within a not so ordinary world
With sources few and far between

Reawakening more often required by the hero
Knowledge is power and insight is clear
Restarting of a story that never once stopped

Swimming in the sea highlights the vacancy of invincibility
Similarly sensed when speaking with you
Terrified to the core, yet giddy

Eager to explore endless possibilities
Petrified of the unknown and beyond controllable prospects
Emancipation from the status quo

Speculation will always exist
With repetitive experience we learn to leverage
To gain strength from a weakness

A being's origin is not a reflection of their outcome
Sincerity of a character's character, flaws and all
Revival of a better being

ENCORE, THE CROWD ROAR

the crowd they cheer and - oh dear
I'm sure I may have just heard a sneer

I thought I might have been in the clear
how wrong I was I fear, they jeer

at times I wish I could just disappear
right here, the atmosphere appears so dreadfully drear

I want to shed a tear, but I don't adhere
near and near, towards my goals I steer

every year, the voices get louder in my ear
I do my best to interfere, but I'm no frontier

if I had the choice I'd still volunteer
I start to hear the cheers grow more severe, how queer

encore - the crowd roar
I dread to be the greatest bore and so I settle the score,

I choose to soar

PART 2

BOYS WILL
BE BOYS

4

a distaste for desire

HUNGER

The lonesome tiger preys across land
looking to pounce on the deer first-hand

Slithering through the grass the snake appears
a movement of their next meal causing sudden veers

Up above, the hawk stalks from the sky
the snake with no idea of its upcoming fate to die

Crocodiles emerging from the lake for their next feast
already targeting an unsuspecting wildebeest

And the spider designs the most beautiful art
a stunning trap to tangle the fly and outsmart

The wolf lurks through the darkness of night
ending the life of the hare remaining out of sight

A cheetah bolts as quick as the flick of the wrist
the starving cat becoming the king of the forest

The chameleon changes the colour of his skin
a survival instinct, now the nearby rock his twin

We do what we have to do to get by
living in this world, eye for an eye

We are led by hunger to succeed and strive
the ultimate life goal is simply to survive

I BOUGHT YOU A MIRROR

Something selfless for the selfish
Pondering what it may take
Infatuated with an image over reality
Convincing me worthy of your presence

A gift for the self-proclaimed gifted
Spending a surplus of my time
Wealth depleted of an irreplaceable currency
In exchange for simple mutual connection

A blindingly shining awakening
Awareness in the reflection of your actions
The perfect attempt for my final plea
I bought you a mirror

PERCEPTIVE DISSONANCE

Perception is reality
Reality is what we know to be true
If knowing to be true is what is defined
Then my interpretation of love in life exists in you

To be considered normal
Conforming to a standard, usual, typical or expected
Is conditioned from our culture
A redefining of our definition can be resurrected

What do I know to be true?
Everything I see, all that I do
As we break down the character traits of our being
Our position shifts in lieu

A table is tangible
Emotions running through my system are not
The senses of human nature
Considered to be an afterthought

My understanding is that our understandings differ
What's normal is normal, to someone who deems it normal
We celebrate individuality as individuals
Yet agree over the idea of becoming conformal

We are but a manifestation of our environment
To describe oneself is to describe what one has been exposed to
We are but fabricated and manipulated beings
With no other choice but to live as we do

Culture is man-made
If holding similar beliefs in unison from inception
Through decades and centuries combined
Then I would never hold dear my perception

GODSPEED

We crossed paths
Intersected each other's stories
On our own individual journeys

We played our roles well
A side character to the main tale
A minor blimp in the major scale

We learnt from each other
Taught lessons to help us on our way
Adding some colour to shades of grey

Filling in the blank
A useful resource for each other
Our wings eventually spread and flutter

And no longer we're in touch
Similar in styles we were sure enough
Two diamonds in the rough

Grateful for the time we had
I hope I planted a memorable seed
And with that, I wish you well

- Godspeed

GARGOYLE GATES

At the foot of the steep winding hill
The gargoyle gates stand powerful and strong
Warily watching over the remote grounds
Seeking prey in that that doesn't belong
Playing warden like a loyal watchdog
The guardians from darkness don't rest
Patrolling the realm for potential destruction
Of stone and marble they stay perpetually abreast
Their great grey wings expand far and wide
Aged horns atop their head made of sharpened rock
Terrifyingly unnerving to even the most evil
Ready to savage intruders and unwanted flock
Many fear the gargoyles are too intense
The walls too high and cinder block thick
But when the walls were down last
Trust was compromised
Leaving no choice but to triple the brick
It's important to realise they'll never attack
The gargoyles sit at the foot of the steep winding hill
Their purpose to protect from all that is tense
Safeguarding for me
In my defence

PLANET EARTH

The grass beneath my feet
Our precious and remarkable land
Looking for the respect it deserves
At mercy to the litter-filled hand

The elixir of the earth
Coming from the wide and wondrous sea
Its lifespan becoming an egg-timer
Filling with plastic and even more harmful debris

Home of all beautiful living creatures
Their existence seen in the mass like a novelty
Co-existing on this planet together
A world free from animal cruelty

A look back at the man in the mirror
Ideas of social justice our implanted botany
A desire for living together harmoniously
The utopia of human equality

PEGASUS

Personality brimming
Of confidence and kindness
Living like it's your full final day
Of your extraordinary life
An immortal winged horse

Never allowing yourself
To lead a little life
When inside you there is so much more
That won't ever go unused
And never will be

Sometimes I think you see yourself
As a dark horse
Unaware of the light you bring
Inspiring me and others to shine
Bright like never seen before

Why do we get all this life
If we don't ever use it?
Why do we get all these feelings
And dreams and hopes
If we don't ever use them?

This transcendent place
Where angels, gods & saints reside
Be enthroned, or live
Is evident in your presence
Doing our best
To enjoy this remarkable ride

In a world of stallions and unicorns
Like lightning to a dark and dreary day
One thing is for sure
You are Pegasus

REGRET OR RELIEF

Be careful what you wish for
The need to have something special
The want for memorable events
Become an unhealthy obsession to the core

And when it's all over
We wonder was it really worth the hype
To be truly good as what it seemed
Achievement of our aspirations redeemed

An underwhelming sense of relief
Questioning of our actions and own intent
A build-up of our expectations
Of which would never have been a belief

Gaining a grasp on the foundation of our motives
Likelihoods of quixotic assumptions
An unconscious cause for upset
The overwhelming feeling of regret

Notions of wanting what we can't or just had
Our desires leading to self-destruction
Disregarding the outcome or aftermath of our actions
Leaving us sombre, and remorsefully sad

THROUGH THE LOOKING GLASS

take a look through
the looking glass and tell me
truthfully, you are proud
of what you see

does the butterfly reflect
on their time beyond the chrysalis
now affecting the velocity
and fluidity of which it flies?

we need not be embarrassed
by who we once were,
but be inspired by
who we are in the midst of becoming

and so I aim to look through
the looking glass with pride
learning from the life lived
a humble caterpillar gone past

dreaming,
of someday unleashing the inner
beauty of my being, that I was
born to bring to life

5

holofernes

THIN ICE

The blistering cold ground
Meets the warmth of my sole
Trembling, steady and slow
Cracks in my assurance become certain

A ticking time bomb
Echoes of pandemonium nearing
Yellow, red, blue or green
Too late to trigger

I drew the short straw
Settled my fate and it's short-lived
Life support to the already lifeless
The camel lays still on the arctic terrain

Eggshells built from the beginning
The indisputable crunching of promises breaking
I continued to walk out to the middle of the lake
Always somehow knowing it was going to fall

Slits to the skin sink deeper
Deafening of the drums
The scars of the landscape disseminate
Shattering from beneath me

DOWN THE LINE

The deceleration of a truth-less oath
A gleam of faith for the futile

Catch you on the flip side
Down the line

Led towards the trail less travelled
Unanimity of an ill-will consensus

We'll meet beyond the bounds and borders
Down the line

I'll sit and wait by the wishing tree
The newest resident of a fool's paradise

On the dark side of the moon
Wishing and waiting for one more time

Down the line

A REGREFUL REGURGITATION

I grab my throat,
in horror and shock
A spewing of honesty
onto your uninvited lap
Immediate penitence
spills into the atmosphere
A look
on my face of disappointment
and upset
I wish,
I could,
and I would
take it back ·
The regretful regurgitation
I couldn't control
Changing everything,
begging to retract
Speaking on how I feel,
an immediate qualm
I convince myself,
that things will get better
past night
A beautiful
misconception
of hindsight

HOLOFERNES

We cross paths in all walks of life
The man, the myth, the legend
The abuser of power, in desperate seek
A cunning breed of sorts

Sitting at the head of the table
Unaware of justice, waiting to be served
A chalice filled with your own
Just desserts

A strong source of self-destruction
The unbeknownst suicide mission
A blissful beheading of ignorance
And the suited execution of selfishness

And again you will lose one's head
Whether it be from me or you
Hunger for retaliation engorged as
What goes around will come swinging with force

SORE LOSER

It's sweet to taste, your bitter failure
Not by some misfortune or even bad luck

Complaining and blaming others for your loss
A fair and square trial, no forfeit in sight

And the days to come filled with morbid regret
Angered easily by a difficult defeat

A sore winner has fallen, what were we to expect?
An attitude less graceful was imminent no less

Deepest sincerity offered towards your defeat
You won't get your way for once, a tough bite to eat

Remembering to not celebrate those you hate
It's easy to become those we don't anticipate

Taken into consideration, I offer my condolences
And better look next time, my sweet sweet inferior

3 WISHES

III

I plea for your respect of one's community alike
Giving consideration to the culture
To those who will and won't cross your path

II

I ask that kindness is given to oneself
That you will tend to and care for the lone flower
And blossom into the greatest burst of bloom

I

I wish for your satisfaction with decisions made
When you close on the final chapter
You will be fulfilled with the choices paged

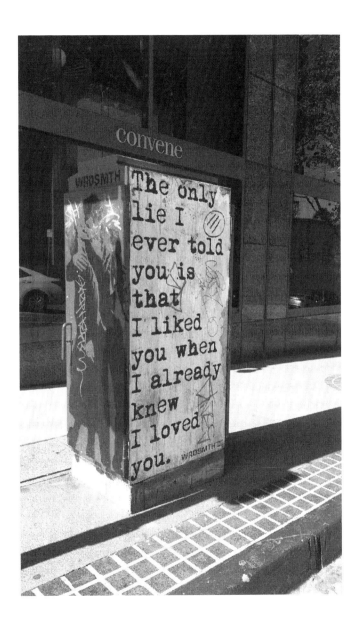

THE BEAUTIFUL MISCONCEPTION OF HINDSIGHT

We look back on the past
Living in a dreamland
Seeing things as better than they were
Life as we once thought we knew

Reminiscing in retrospect
Embarrassed of ourselves, what a shame
Holding us accountable for our actions
Admired apparitions running in parallel

Hindsight, the beautiful misconception
Planting flowers to the badlands
We add colour to the outlines of history
A rainbow dazzling through what was
Once a storm ridden sky

THE BLANK STAINED CANVAS

I pull out my blank stained canvas
And try to wipe away the marks
Diluting the damage of previous remarks

The stains stand stubborn
Hidden some and evidently present at times
Regardless, I carry on

A flicker of my brush
Starting to lay new foundations
My longing vision still strongly in mind

Layers thicken as time stretches
I hang my painting pride of place
Knowing what's hidden still behind the walls

FORBIDDEN FRUIT

A red apple glitters
Like a single ornament
Among the busy green leaves
With an insatiable hunger burning,
Alive with temptation to take it in my fist
And watch the seeds bleed down
My outreached arm towards my naked feet
Nestled neatly within the grass, six feet above
My future, if I were to take a single bite
And reveal beneath the rotting flesh that lies beneath
You're desirable
You're destructible
You're tempting
Forbidden fruit

I swiftly turn my back
Away from the beaten track,
Returning towards again,
the promising garden path
I step into the glistening swimming pool
Relief from the heat, fully submerged and cool
Roles reverse as I pull myself back up to surface
My own sparkling impulses now flattening
Diamonds dripping, clinging to my bare skin
Salt water on a sweltering hot day
Your desirable
Your destructible
Your tempting
Forbidden fruit

6

here's to you, kiddo!

CHASING DRAGONS

I want to have the shiniest car
red, silver, green or gold
as long as it's fast and loud and low down
to the ground so when people see it
and hear the sound
they will know it's me coming

The house I will have is going to be huge
with a big massive roof that towers over the brick completely
and to get to my house will be this long winding road that's so
long
it would nearly give you a headache
with lamp posts the whole way to the door that are beaming
up from the stone floor
people are going to wonder who lives there

My wife will be beautiful beyond belief
and my kids are going to think I'm the greatest dad ever
because I'm going to play with them all the time even when I'm
tired
on their games or whatever they have then in the future
like robots or things that fly in the sky
I just want to be that guy that everybody will see
and turn to each other in jealousy to say
he must got it so good

NOSTALGIA

A moment of unanticipated transit
Sparking our memory of a place we have already been

Detecting images of visible light, of likeness
With electrical nerve-impulses striking us as once again seen

The assertion of odour molecules clouding the air
An accumulative haze of a previously-accustomed scene

Being able to identify a taste all that familiar
Playing reminder to a time few and far between

A perceived sound through detected vibrations
Forcefully guiding us towards a remembrance held keen

Activating pressure receptors held in the skin
A conscious contemplation of a fondling convene

The unwilling traveller transported through space and time
Guilty of a retrospective crime of what has or could have been

HOLLYWEIRD

The glorious sun
Lining the streets like glitter
Beaming through windows as fiery torches
Heating up the paths and plants

The trees extended 100 feet high
Fronds growing from the crown wide
Crashing against each other in the wind
Swaying back and forth in a dreamy-like fashion

The pools are as deep as the trees are tall
An underwater dream world I've dreamt in sleep
Swimming in slow motion, strokes and all
Under the water nobody can hear you singing your songs

The streets and the sky are at war
Together they're counting who holds the most stars
Surrounded by inspiration and beauty
Remembering to count your own ones too

And everyone there has their own unique style
Pink mow-hawks spiked to the sky
Skating down the polished pavement
Kickflips and coffee all day long
Every corner I'll pass it's clear
Seventh heaven will be a place smack bang right here
Overlooking the sign that this will be normal
Fitting in nicely will be even more weird

DOLL BOY

People laugh when they see
He, who is playing with the 'girls' toys
Making up imaginative stories and playing free

Quietly brushing their hair
And putting on the latest fashion
The boy and these dolls a godforsaken pair

Chronicling lives with complex tales
Throwing them from the shelf to the blazing fire
A streak of masculinity veils

Interested in castles and lands of magic
Keeping himself enchanted
Elders look on feeling less than tragic

Dolls won't make him any less of a gent
Looking past the standard stereotypes and you'd see
A boy who simply could not be more content

THE DARKNESS

A sweet embrace
Ignites the darkness
Freeing me from my fears
Flashes of complete starkness

The monster under my bed
Is trying to outdo and fool me
Transforming into a great big anaconda
Catching my jolting leg as I attempt to flee

The only light source that of the bathroom bulb
As it's past midnight and my bladder full
The demon at the bottom of the stairs waiting
For me to open the door for him to grab and pull

A hooded fellow hiding around the corner
Ready to pounce making his identity known
To use and do with me as he pleases
Of my bones he'll make his throne

Faces in the frames follow me with their eyes
Their features melting the longer they stare
Sprinting and panting, I bolt on by
Through the crack of the door I feel their glare

A martyr to my own imagination
Worry and voodoo considered sisters not twins
Of my own mind I easily fall victim
Befriending the unknown for all my sins

ANOTHER SLICE OF TOAST

Jolting closed the door
Keeping out the rain
The wet seeped through to my socks
My feet cold again
Treading through the river-like town
A journey that felt like it would never end
Through the blistering cold we fought the wind
Puddles aplenty with my pockets zipped

Fresh cotton and linen line my skin
Warming up now and feeling myself again
I hear the kettle let out it's roar
Bundled onto the couch tired and sore
Asking when's dinner my stomach is empty
A clutter of cups I hear something coming
Hot chocolate and toast
My tiny belly lets out its last rumble

The television volume spikes for the ads
Causing ructions to my unintended slumber
I toss and turn on the comfortable couch
Bundled into what feels like a kangaroo pouch
Warm and snug I switch sides
In the process making some exaggerated noise
In a hope it'll be clear that I'm awake
Another slice of toast she'll know to make

GLADIATOR IN TRAINING

Skidding across the great hall
Trying to anticipate the next move
Like a ninja stuck to the wall
A gladiator in training

Climbing the mountainous chair
Sweat dripping from my temple
The red gladiator in complete despair
On my tail the entire course

Tip-toeing across the tight rope
The lava bubbling beneath
My opponent beginning to interlope
Losing my balance out of sheer panic

And then my final match
The coach who taught me everything
This chick is training to hatch
Making my best attempt to triumph

Now the graduated contender
In search of his own in Shangri-La
With goals made up of absolute splendour
The student has become the master

LEARNING

A promise to making smarter decisions
Removing emotions from the situation
Waiting until tomorrow
And knowing my own worth

The extra effort to be honest, but kind
Understanding that perception is reality
Awareness of the long-term effect of my actions
While minding my own business

That I have a choice to be miserable or be motivated
Identifying my vices, and limiting them
Utilising available resources to the best of my ability
And to leverage my responses effectively

I'm going to listen and ask more
Talk less about myself
To prioritise my privacy as modesty is sexy
I will appreciate and create more art

Needing to understand the difference
between want and need
Are you on the right path for where you want to be?
Practising to the best of my ability self-control
Asking questions like 'how is this really effecting me?'

Happiness is not a final destination
If it takes less than a minute, do it now
To live life a little less hectic
Plans should only be seen as a suggestion

To be more proactive and less reactive
Nobody else really cares about your goals
Turning your thoughts into ideas and actions
I need to step up for the starring role

Every day I am learning
Picking off apples from the knowledge tree
And if I continue to nurture my appetite
Then I am simply the best that I will ever be

EST. 1993

I still love you
Like I did yesterday
Like I did when you got me through the hard times
I may not always say it
But I do
I do

When the good times come
I'm drunk on you
Slurring my words, the nights move fast
In the blink of an eye, I hardly remember the day before
But I do
I really do

Cause together we've been through it
And I've said things about you I didn't mean
But after all this time, you know I'm really not that mean
Just sometimes you frustrate me
You do
You really do

At the end of it all, when push comes to shove
It still hurts me to think,
No matter what, at that time I actually think
Everything in this world holds a sell-by date
Even you
Even you too

So I try not to take you for granted
And take you for what you are
Day by day, I'll aim to take in each moment
No matter what lies ahead for us
I still love you
I do

PART 3

WAR OF
THE WORLDS

7

through the crack
of the emerald stone

BOOMERANG

Do what you love and love what you do
And the world will come boomeranging back

The laws of cause and affect
If initiated correctly, full circles to you

An equivalent and opposite reaction for every action
Benefiting from the garden of which you sowed

Living by the principle of an unfulfilled prophecy
The deeds and words will soon recur

To celebrate the coming of the Prodigal Son
Because once lost, he is now found

And just like a boomerang If to leave once more
Without a shadow of a doubt, I'll return once again

SUMMER SOLSTICE

A celebration of the sun
Utter joy spread and exposed to everyone
True representation of ascension

New seasons showcasing immense beauty
Ushering in the new light of nature's bounty
Awareness to all the good around me

Stopping to the smells of roses, and I will
Speculation of a right move
I suddenly know to be true

Longing for you in the dark nights
Knowing you would come, impatient still
We had the stars, you and I

A time of new beginnings with more to unfold
Illumination triumphs over darkness
Light of my life

THE LAST-BORN TOD

What does it mean to be the last-born Tod?
Holder of the pen to the future kin
The creator of life to continue a legacy on
Or the God of death to dwindle it all

Difficult it is, to imagine an unwinding road
To imagine just how far back the history goes
To see each face of ancestry gone
Watching over as I carry the crest strong

Walking through the forest filled with fear
Swinging the axe to the tree so greatly grown
Year to year, the branches and roots stemmed long
A fall from grace, pinned as all my fault

Then again, the halter of heritage may not sound so bad
To bequest the power to put it all to an end
Knighted for eternity as the final bearing progeny
O, what a wondrous victory that would be

BIG 'OL PRIVATE JOKE

To be born and bred in deep green roots
Is to be in on one big 'ol private joke
A kinsmanship and community of a different kind
Pointing in hysterics as the world goes by
A deeper understanding into the depths of the world
With an acuteness and wit unmatched by neighbouring foes
A tiny land with a magnificent footprint among our toes
Duplicated but never replicated, never a truer word
Cause everyone wants to be in on the antic
Every year without fail, they pledge their allegiance
To us, the most wanted and claimed group there was
Coming from a place where "No Irish allowed!"
To turning rivers and buildings green in a plea for consent
Cheering among us not knowing what's really happening
And the world can continue to try to take part
At the end of the day, we know what we know
We will continue to go about our small island days
Making waves in the world and laughing along the way

EMERALD

Rich and distinct
High of value
And soothing some

The embodiment of patience
A compassionate carer
Mental clarity and focus

Freshness and vitality
Unconditional love, unity full
The bringer of luck

Good fortune a plenty
Reasoning and spirituality
And wisdom galore

Rarer than rare
The deepest of hue
My pact to you

HOMEGROWN LOVE

The curtain dances in the draft as the wind creeps in
What feels like a beam of fire freeing the world from sin
To the left, the tiny red light on standby shines
In my sanctuary of warmth stacking the pillows high
The comforting heat a spell, making me drift on by

And the ticking clock in competition for distraction
The duck feather duvet sound proofing from impaction
The wood is creaky and conducts its recital
Funny from such a sound, the composer so blatantly obvious
For the unwilling audience remaining oblivious

The window gazing out into the world going by
And the stars and street lights stare right back and spy
I switch over, flipping the pillow to its colder side
The familiarity of belongings, surrounded in the well-known
With a grown appreciation for home

MOTHER

Something to be said about a mother's touch
The most beautiful of spirit on this godly earth
A powerful creature, the creator of life
Supreme being, of divinity high

A nurturing care, comparable to none
The almighty minder, our mothering mum
Loving and kindness to all coming her way
The presence of sense to all madness led stray

But mother can be a sensitive soul
And is ageing as days go by and getting old
We must do what we can to keep her fresh
And as our duty, out of clear respect

The deed of life is unrepayable for us
Doing our best, being conscious of our tread
To be sensitive, kind and giving back
Look after and keep safe the cradle of life

TIR NA NÓG

Legend says there is a place, beyond the western sea
Appropriately crowned, the land of the young
A place where age was never a fear
With skies bluer than blue and trees even more green

Where on land and sea, white horses run free
Across the golden shores of Tír na nÓg
A magical place of fawns and fairies
Residing among the few living harmoniously

Through the morning mist, the sunshine rose
Every day, what felt like summer solstice
The hills grew high and the grass long
A place some couldn't even think to dream at all

Not always I make it to Tír na nÓg in a day
As often creatures come trying to pull me away
Tripping and stumbling to make it across the hill
Every morning, my aim is even just to try and see it still

NECTAR

He sought to make an impact
Find fulfilment out of life
Chasing a cure to mortality
Concocting a potion of sorts
From the words spewing
Out of his mind
He drank the nectar
And now he's drunk on poetry
In an out of body experience
A master of mystery
Graduating to the highest degree
With no intention to stop this high
Because he's not giving back his wings
After he's finally learnt to fly
He chugs it down his thirsty gob
An elixir for his rotting flesh
His vision for the future
Quenched
Sealed with a promising kiss
Immortality
His first and final wish

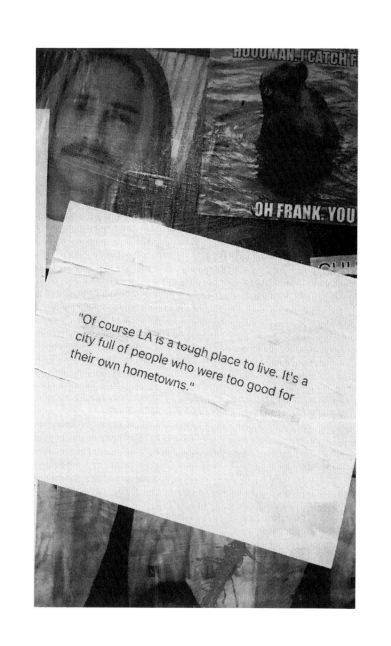

"Of course LA is a tough place to live. It's a city full of people who were too good for their own hometowns."

8

the bull & the rooster

XXVI

Another the wiser
Wondering if I've grown stronger
On to the next one
No rest for the wicked

Clasping my boots
Preparing for the next battle
Releasing a sigh of relief
We made it this far

Knowledge is power
Ignorance is naivety
Calmness held to a higher regard
And silence golden

Respect and gratitude shall flourish
Self-control is arduous
Growth is imminent
I will be stronger

TOUGH LOVE

I hand you the pill
You find tough to swallow
I tried my best to spoon feed you
Spitting it out every time still

Tough love

I offer it honest and upfront
You reject, again
Leaving a bad taste in your mouth
I willingly force it upon you blunt

Tough love

I hope my vision will be clear someday
The struggles I've tried to make you see
My efforts in leading you down the right path
By walking away

Tough love

WHAT IT MEANS TO BE A CHAMPION

What does it mean to be a champion?
The superior, undefeated and truly out of this world
To be a champion of myself
Supporting and rooting for my own success
Allowing yourself to be confident but not cocky
Graciously outdoing my own efforts and abilities
Being an example of humbleness and modesty in victory
Level-headed and down to earth
If I am to wear the crown with honour
It will be because I have outdone and become my own successor
So, what does it really mean to be a champion?
To be supporting, challenging and becoming victorious
Both for and against one's self

I WILL

I will nourish my mind
Be empathetic to my thoughts
And a therapist to my own feelings

I will build my body strong
Assemble a shrine of health
Something of which to be worshipped

I will fuel my spirit
And promise to pray for my soul
Being true to my inner being always

I will cater to my whole self
Creating circumstances which to burgeon
To the moon and back

THE STUBBORN SEA CAPTAIN

There once was a stubborn sea captain
Sailing through the storm wearing proudly his gold clothes-pin

He liked to do things his own way
No member of crew on board could be of any help or have a say

Opinionated a plenty, on how the seas should be tackled
The talents of the crew on the operation of the ship left shackled

The stubborn sea captain passed judgement on his pirates
Definitive statements in passing on their character often lead to riots

Cause it was clear to him that no one could be as good as he
Yet none would get the chance to even see if they could be

A perfectionist with an ego as tall as the mast
No room for rigging as self-considered the best in all deck's past

The stubborn sea captain couldn't see that they were only trying to help
Getting involved and playing their part with the deadly storms dwelt

When one day he finally discovered the woes of his ways
The maps towards his treasures became much less of a maze

GOODWILL CUNNING

People look to the fox and call him cunning
Shrewd and slick in their ways
The dog skilled in achieving one's ends by deceit
Preying and planning and left lurking in the street

To be considered cunning is less than favourable
Devious some, in seek of defeat
Crafty and cute, and not in the good way
The artful pup often led astray

A credible misunderstanding of determination
Or a strong-willed animal approach to success
With purposeful intent
Useful traits to progress could remain unspent

But if the end justifies the means
Good outcome excusing the wrongs to initiate it
Fancy footwork used to entertain rather than bluffing
That to me, is goodwill cunning

WAR OF THE WORLDS

In the midst of smoke and debris
I rise up from my knee
Getting my balance and wits about me
Slowly taking in my surroundings

The landscape swamped with grey
A bleak dark red sky conceals the fray
Blood shed is imminent
Playing witness to the battle at play

Clashing, of what seems like a thousand swords
A battle so otherworldly
Even the planets are colliding
I fall to avoid the arrows shot forward

In the mix up and scuffle of bodies aplenty
Bullets swerve past in this great manic frenzy
Utter destruction to the universe known
The rival cavalries disputing with blows

In the darkened day, it's clear in sight
A bull and a rooster
Scrapping through the night
Wounding each other 'til death is ripe

To my left, a pack and a troop
Tearing one another arm and limb
What looks to be a fight for the right
To lead, to seek, to take centre flight

The participants grow wounded
Carnage inevitably escalating
To an almighty melodramatic climax
An inauguration of the winner leads on

When the smoke has cleared
I am the last standing
Hostility has entered it's hibernation
I take a deep breath and sit in reflection

And just as I begin to enjoy the calm
The serenity of the land at last
Grateful, for my now clear head
I see the battalion rise again from the dead

SUNFLOWER FIELDS

Garden of Eden
With a population of one
And the thousands of seeds I've sowed
Sprouting into flowers imitating the sun

An aim for adoration
Across acres of grass my allegiance loyal
I walk the lengths of the land watering daily
Building a heavens made for longevity

My planting regime to be admired
A substantial dedication for the roots of my soil
The fountain of youth, I hope to build
This life worth living won't go unfulfilled

Laying in the fields of my legacy
Protective of my offspring, quite literally
I have and will reach the rill of Nirvana
My promised land

THE GAME OF LIFE

The game of life
Is never fair
The game of life
Is rarely square
It's the circle of life
In which we play
To find the meaning of life
The name of the game
And so we chase;
The snakes and the ladders
We learn to embrace
We learn to deal with what
We are subject to face
The hand in which we are dealt
We are succumb to accept
And how we deal with the blows
From off our feet we're swept
To win the game
And finally,
feel that we are free
We have to take the lemons
We've been handed
And plant a lemon tree
We join forces;
And make allies along the way
Together hand in hand
Is how it is made to be played
Because in the game of life
There is no guarantees

As long as we lead with kindness
It doesn't matter
What anyone else believes
So make sure to pick up and play
The game of life
See what happens
And roll the dice
But always remember
That everything in life
Will come
With a price

9

wasteland

BACK TO CALIFORNIA

When the sun sets in the west
I'll go back to California
Laying leisurely and still on the sandy beach
Silently admiring the diamonds of the sparkling sea

Blinded by the light of tranquillity and peace
I can see the world from here
A viewpoint I will everlastingly take advantage of
This, my happy hunting ground

In the history books of my family name
I'll be christened Icarus
Forever flying too close to the sun
Always your Angeleno

And when the sun rises in the east
Like clockwork
Drenching the days ablaze with orange
You'll know where to find me

DAVID

Here before
And here more will come
The past is my present
A situation of inseparability
Experiencing this moment in time
An intimacy of crossed paths
Destiny unfolding through paper pools

They say life imitates art
Here, I will attest
My own animate existence knowing the score
Material works are more than an influence
In the beginning, there was only art
And nature it's guided disciple

Reincarnation of a unique kind
The living unified through resurrection
Through the rebirth of story, not soul
Consider this my coronation as the second king
The hierarchal samsara
And to those who will come after me
Well, here's looking at you

WHEN THE SUN SETS ON SUNSET

When the sun sets on Sunset
We watch the fall of fragile man as the seven crawl

From seeking beyond one's need
Believing that of which a requirement to succeed

To those who conduct a comparison of sorts
Sinking slowly into the sea of green

Acting intensely in their most convincing role yet
The scale grounded on validation, burying them underneath

And no concern held for the apathetic
As the weeds will succumb the disengaged buds

And we can't not hear the loud roar of the lion
Echoing a spurn-filled sorrowful plea, if you listen closely

Retaliation is a matter of time to the vengeful
In a vicious cycle of violent poetic justice

As for the self-diagnosed deficient
Alas, the insatiable look after themselves

And then there are those who have learned to conquer control
Frivolously dancing on the moon not afraid to fall

PICTURE PERFECT

Living a fantasy
The immaculate impression
Life as we know it
A flight of fancy

Pressure makes diamonds
A confinement of the mind
What is supposed to be
Crumbling through vain expectation

Reaching for the moon
Storming the ladder
Desperate to simply be
Building castles in the air

Rewarding of the highest efforts
If indefatigably chasing
A life made that others will see
Picture perfect

POOLSIDE PT. II

Submerging from the dreamy depths
Panting, heaving, gasping
Satiety, starving for more
Plummets delving through the portrayal

Far beyond wild
Levelled up ten-fold
If happiness is power, then me
The most powerful man in the world

Mesmerising sisters work hand and foot
White frocks frolic with the wind
Rosé diluting rapidly
O, what a fortunate misfortune

A knowing touch
Grounds haunted with history
Wise winks met with a simultaneous smile
Alive again

FERRIS WHEEL

In the pit of my stomach
I foresee my prophecy steering south
When an eery silence swamps the surroundings
A breathy snigger pierces the atmosphere
A longing look overflowing in let-down
Is followed up with a slow modest smirk

The built walls of frustration
Annihilated through the winds of affirmation
When the storm of insecurity finally strikes the village
The conjuration of assurance casts over the sky
And when I start to look back up
The kaleidoscope of butterflies fly free

THE BALLAD OF PEG ENTWISTLE

Dear darling Peg
And now the Lord with thee
Blessed is the passion to which you lived
And sacrificed in the name of your art

To be remembered in perpetuity
A desire to succeed held to the highest
Alive through a Great Depression
The irony of which a humorous affair

We are all afraid, and often cowardly
A slave to our own expectations
Conscious of every one of our actions
And the effects they have on those around us

Now, since that historic day in Fall
A determined stride through Beachwood Drive
Thy Kingdom has finally come
And your legacy forever alive

WASTELAND

Another sole's treasure
Cheating death, the life raft
Sailing and shoring

Bumps and bruises aplenty
Thrown to the wolves
There are two sides to every sword

Experience to be admired
The card-less sleeve
Image of the invisible

Beauty to the imperfections
Surface level scenarios
Looking beyond the landscape

You may say I'm pushing up daisies
I see lilacs out of the dead land

IN THE GARDEN OF ALLAH

Buried beneath the normalcy
By a concrete commercial society
The lost city, out of plain sight
Where love once shared shall lie
Sank, to the bottom of the Black Sea
Where myths are born, legends die
A summer's kiss, middle of July
We will live forever,
In the Garden of Allah
Our den of debauchery denied
Put to rest in eternal sunshine
Alongside an old life well-lived
Of mine
And I don't want to give it all away
But temptation often got the best of me
Never getting to say our goodbyes
So now when I hear our song
I no longer sing the lines,
I smile, and I daydream -
I daydream about the good times
I daydream about all the too-coincidental signs
I daydream about the never ending wine;
the dinners shared on Hollywood and Vine
I daydream about the golden era
And just how bright it truly shined
Put to rest now in eternal sunshine
Alongside an old life well-lived
Once mine

II

BEACH
BOY

"The real voyage of discovery consists not in seeking new lands but in seeing with new eyes."

— Marcel Proust

1

the sun

JACK OF ALL TRADES

It's time for you to meet the Jack of All Trades
Who could play the Queen of Hearts and even the King of
Spades

A man who can fit to whichever mould he needs
Whatever is required of him, constantly aiming to please

The hats he wears differ in size, matter and style
Each holding its own responsibilities, expectations and trial

Someone you can rely on to get the job done
Remaining content, as long as he still gets to see the sun

The thing about the boy is he can be anyone you want him to be
The greatest of actors, not yet trained academically

Each to their own, people hold their perceptions of Jack
His awareness of these differing narratives, often difficult to
knack

Everyone believes to know him, this well-grounded guy
But do they know –

That all he has ever wanted to do is fly

WELCOME TO THE BEACH CLUB

Welcome to the beach club
The finest in all the land
This exclusive destination fabricated from sea and sand
A manifestation of this world at hand

Welcome to the beach club
Where the proletariat and aristocrats cross paths
A place that through the summer the wealth resides
And the less well-off more often than not thrown to the side

Welcome to the beach club
Where the lines in the sand are clearly blurred
Of those who are relatively happy, and those who are sad
The poor unseemly sane, and the rich are even more mad

Welcome to the beach club
A destination that contains no truth or certainty
Conversations held here are conceited and figural
And sex on the beach is something even more literal

Welcome to the beach club
Where those who are undeserving are clearly not welcome
An unrightfully prejudice, exclusive and elitist place
Existence of which in this day and age, our fall from grace

Welcome to the beach club
Here, perception is the highest valued currency
The lines of perspective never meet, skewed with despair
As we're reminded once more, that nothing in life is truly ever
fair

HANDING OVER MY HEART

A permanent commitment
Resistance to my own choices
Second guessing myself some more
Another step towards self-declared victory
Creaks loudening on the hard-wood floor
And finally - everyone's going to know the score

In my hands my beating heart
Atmospheric hypertension
I'm used to tending to the beat of my own drum
Heavy pounding and tougher thumps
Sensitive, and even slippery some
A nerve-wrecking transplant analogised to none

My darkest fears forming a clot
The weight of my world in my trembling hands
Releasing it free from my grip with a sigh of relief
No longer held captive under my chest
Torn from my limbs as the ink drips with grief
From life's tree, sprouted this beautiful leaf

In the act of this vulnerable exchange
The blood begins to splatter across the floor
Seeping through the cracks, suddenly considered ceaseless art
My existence becoming everlastingly immortal
Losing control was always going to be the hardest part
In this operation, of handing over my heart

SUN BUM

Every day
I seek the warmth of the sun
I am selfish
Often driven by this desire
And equally at times gluttonous some
My longing for the light sometimes overbearing
Sacrificing other opportunities
Which become a loss
These built-up bricks become walls
Holding out any other opportunity cost
Because I am blinded by the light
Laser-focused and losing sight
On the glorious radiance of summer's daylight
It's not a bad thing to find what you love
A reason to keep going
To make it through the dark nights,
And the at times, even darker day
As I strive to beam in the sun all day
But behind the science of every sundial
Is the significance of scale
The equilibrium of our priorities
And every now and again
The importance of a little hail

THE HIGH ROAD
(HAIKU)

Often hard to reach
The high road's summit is
Heavenly sublime

I AM AN ISLAND

I am an island
And that is okay
I have grown and become sheltered
In some and every which way
I don't consider myself remote
But more simply just astray
From the mainland's ever-expanding bay
Don't let me be misunderstood
I will always welcome each element
As well as the sea, the waves,
The wind, the stars, the sand
It is not an exclusive or elitist place
I'll stress to say
I am simply just an island
Flowing with the way the wind blows
Operating on my own accord
Here is home to indigenous thoughts
I enjoy the peace this way of life brings
The promised land promised
Is a stones throw in the ocean
An island in the sea, out past the bay
And from the mainland's touch
Slowly, I move further,
and further away

RUBBING SHOULDERS

I'm getting closer to the life I want
Rubbing shoulders with the other kind
I sit, I watch, I observe
Try to understand their movements and actions
How they got to where they are
A place in life that often seems oh so sublime.

Through the valley,
I still have so much further left to go
Taking any direction where I can
Following the signs that I have come across
And in my own interpretation of them
They don't always come across all that clear at all.

The people that I meet along my journey
I try to take from them what I can get
Sourcing the information that I can
Listening, and learning contently and calm
Sometimes, only just watching from afar
Absorbing the tips and tricks that I can take and run.

Cause if I'm rubbing shoulders with the right kind
I want to make sure I remain resourceful and smart
Taking full advantage of the surroundings I've been presented
with
Grateful for these close encounters to explore the others' mind
Figuring out the path to get there myself, on my own grind.

A DOLLAR

What would you do for a dollar?
Would you let a baby cry?
Would you deprive somebody of an opportunity,
and never tell them why?
Would you take another's life?
Would you commit atrocity or crime?
Would you wipe yourself of your dignity,
lose all your respect and simply sigh?
Would you sell your soul to the devil?
Would you give away your time?
What are you willing to sacrifice in your life,
in order just to get by?
Would you partake in treason?
Would you get involved with fraud?
What are the lengths we are willing to take,
or even willing to try?
What would you do for a dollar?
I want to understand what we are capable of
Yet I truly don't mean to pry,
I just want to know if we would still be able
When all is said and done,
to look ourselves in the eye.

SANDCASTLE

All I want is a home, with a view of the sea
I've even had a look
A place where we can be happy
Cause I've peeped the ending of this book

So you go scoop some water for the moat
I'll stay here and mind the land
Working together endlessly
On this castle made of sand

And I hope to the heavens it'll stand tall
Through all the wind that's sure to come
Our home out here among the dunes
To the shore we will have swum

This House of Kings may as well be made of bricks
These walls are solid as a rock
Cause we're the foundation of this château de sable
Impossible to knock

LONG DAYS IN THE SUN

Too much of a good thing
Sometimes seems like never enough
Until it can be too late to see
The evening chill coming breezing in
And the regret of overindulgence sets in

The realisation introduced to us only by hindsight
As the skies, clouds and stars gather
The elements join forces
Eventually pushing away the sun
And only then,
We can finally see the damage done.

SHADOWS

4am in the middle of the night
A shadow caught the corner of my eye
Jumping out of my own skin
Nearly sent into an early grave
It was just a jumper hanging off the door
So I pulled it hard
and went back to rest

That very next day
My mind was put to test
I couldn't get that damn jumper
Out of my mind
How frightened I was
By something so silly
And the power and control it had over me

What did I even expect it to be?
I wasn't even sure
So that very next evening
I made sure my room was comfortably bright
I especially made sure every garment was
Propped away in their proper place and out of sight
And slept like a baby the entire night

2

the moon

9 LIVES

Every now and then I think of the struggles
we've had, and how we thought the world would eat us up
and I continue to look back, eternally and remorsefully glad

The people I dearly miss, the one's I've passionately kissed
lovers that are now considered strangers, to me,
and this new life that I am living since they once existed within it

Gathered groups of pals collected, that were ultimately
cast aside, not all by choice or permanently, I insist to add
with rogue time travelers appearing once again in modern times

The weighing pressures we've previously succumb to, and falling
victim to what we thought would hold us back, heightened ideas
and exaggerated outcomes we feared would arrive, never coming
to pass

Worries we never felt we'd be free from, held captive of our own
biggest fears, fearing for the future, and what was inevitably to
come as if we held no control in what could yet, and still can, be
done

Every role we ever embraced has been a building block of who
we were, are, and becoming, each one we wondered, whether it
would stick, and survive, and outlast the other eight

These contradicting and contrasting versions of me, defined
traits contain multitudes and differ from mind to mind, seen as
this person I once was, to those who only knew me then and
there

In the mix of our lives, this current version of who I am, is just as fluid as those before, not knowing if this my final form, deep down knowing a greater evolution will most definitely derive

You could say that I am carrying, that I am possibly with child, brewing the next version of me, the latest upgrade of my psyche at full-term, waiting to birth another of my many cherished lives

SOMEONE'S CHILD

Do you know that girl you work to shame
The one who's name you fail to frame?
A woman for whom you'd simply die
To secretly lie beside
Do you know she's someone's child?

The quiet guy minding his own time
Keeping to himself, out of harm's way
Who can't ever pass your presence without
Some wise input for you to say
Do you care he's someone's child?

What about the people who mean no harm?
Ones you'll never come or care to understand
Going about their life, their own kind of style
Called to court forcefully to face your trial
Do you mind they're someone's child?

Should we work to care as less as those people
And drown out the urge to pursue a person's motive
Trying to understand the actions of an inflated ego.
I wonder, if pride is held so high while we roam the wild
And if you remember, you too, are someone's child.

MANTICORE

There is much to be said about the company in which we keep
Those whose time we spend like currency
In exchange for ideas, with opinions reaped
Walking into the bar they steadily arrive
Leaving more than an impression, this impressionable five

The fire breathing dragon is the first in the door
Contributions to conversations more often heated
This great winged creature,
With wildfire we were normally greeted.
And as time went on, things stayed much the same
My own breath beginning to spark its very own flame

A werewolf claws his way through the entryway
Marking his territory through the darkened door
Friendly but still, growling at times.
Occasionally letting out an aggressive roar
Spontaneous reactions let out in spur
With each howl heard, I felt my limbs start to grow fur

I grew concerned when my forehead began to sprout a horn
Growing several feet long as time went on and on
Eagerly listening to these stories told.
Brought to us, from the perspective of this great unicorn
Galloping through myths and magical tales,
Our minds captivated, sworn free from scorn

To the left, there was the most beautiful mermaid laying around,
On the ground, of which she made a glistening pool
Dripping water as each tale was told
Audiences forming pulling up the next stool
Her stories enchanting as long as her tale,
As time went on, my skin began to scale

It wasn't long until I felt my owns limbs change
From my body I once knew, I became estranged
Unbeknownst to myself I was now somebody new
As the centaur spoke, he joked of his specific woes
Surrounded by all kinds of beasts,
This new creature rose

So, what was left of little old me?
The naive audience member listening free
Taking it all in even more than I thought
A transformation over time, I never needed nor sought
Out the door, I was a man no more
Instead, my very own breed of a manticore

WASHINGTON SQUARE PARK

One last trip around the block
Finishing our final victory lap inside the park
The course was blind-siding
And the finishing line untimely stark
The end is inevitable, and we both know
It's goodbye to the warmth of the summer sun,
and hello to bitter winter snow

We shall let our tears dry another day
And think of the times that have since past
All the moments spent side by side
Together alone, we are, at last.
Through the highs and lows of the race
We finally found our privacy
At the close, in this very public place

The birds gather around our feet
Picking away at what is left of our crumbs
Our supercut now soundtracked
By the sounds of the NYU students and their drums
And right here, laid out on the grass, we shall lay
Our memory forever etched into the nearby bench
Among the trees, the leaves, the litter and the bark

Here then, now and forever,
At Washington Square Park.

SAME PAGE OF A DIFFERENT BOOK

You have your say
And I have mine
And we will continue to dance
This magnetically charged tangle
And let it untwine.
You dip, I catch
I flip, you twirl
Our energies displayed
Across the stage floor.
Passion, the only choreography
We happen to know by heart
Frolicking through deafening silence
To the sound of our own songs
To the rhythm of our finely tuned tunes
It is made very clear to recognise
Just like the man of science and the man of faith
If anyone was to simply take a look
That those two are on the same page
of a different book

ALIEN BEHAVIOUR

(HAIKU)

In the eyes of small minds
Is going against the grain
So other worldly?

TWO WHITE PAINT PATCHES ON THE ROOF

Clear signs of a story untold
Symbols
Of life that was once lived
Here, but back then
The tale of which they would tell
Two little white paint patches on the roof
Igniting my imagination
Here, and now
The possibilities unravel through the night
How did they come to be?
What chapter of their love story that those were born
Perhaps, maybe it was even something more dull
Like that of a burst pipe
But I simply do not care.
Because I am hopeful
Here, and hopefully later
That those who will come after us
May look up and see our those of our own
Two little white paint patches on the roof
And wonder
Curious if love was a part of this story untold
If it had any part in their creation
And they will, and it did

THE PRIDE PARADE

Finger on the pulse
On the trigger of change
Edging ever so close to glory
Dodging our demise by an inch each time.
Please tell my mom I love her
If it ever comes to it,
If I don't get one last chance
If she never gets to watch me have my very first dance.

Because not so long ago we had no voice
No right to speak, no space to talk
Don't ask, don't tell!
And now here we are, still having to walk
In this rebellion for rights and respect
Storming into the sun, and out of the shade
We will fight back year after year to come, and then some
At the pride parade

GHOST TOWN

I walk the streets of this once familiar town
Only, it's winter now
With every step forward, I seem to move back in time
Back to a period of my life when you were to have worn
The crown
But the queen of this castle has well and truly resigned
Now this distant derelict kingdom
Is nothing, but a ghost town.
The paths are lifeless and pale
With a chilling air sending shockwaves through my spine
Every now and then, I think of how our lives could have been
What could have happened
What we should have never seen.
I can't help but wonder as I walk these streets
Would the leaves of these trees surrounding me still be green,
Livelier than they are now
Than this deathly brown
If you were still to wear the crown.
But that was a time in my life which was led by a lie
I was never fit to rule the kingdom I was offered
That part of me has died
Overcome, reflective, yet content with the outcome,
I am a different person roaming through
this unfamiliar ghost town
And in the sorrows for my old self,
Still, I cannot help but drown.

ROOM 10

Here we are again
Where reality feels imaginary
Here, in the midst of room 10
Peggy Lee serenades of black coffee
As we take a fitting sip to the soaring sounds
Heard within the 5 o clock shadows
Of the dimly lit grounds
Stepping through time, in search of the pool and cottages
The early morning moonlight guiding our way
In what is rightfully now, our playground
Roaming the castle walls, we have succumbed to
Infatuated in the idea of those who have come before us
Walking the walk, hand in hand
We are creating our own history
As they once were.
The history that reeks the halls
The faded carpets littered with tales of folklore
In this transcendent place,
The castle on the hill still stands true against time
Where the damaged reputations of stars lie,
Many of which here, have come to die
In the darkened corners, where secret romances thrive
Thinking of how lucky that we have come to be
And of those who stumbled across these same carpets
Creating their own movies, in which they had starred
Falling deeper and deeper in love
As we now are.

YOUNG SICK BACCHUS

I gathered together my greatest collection of fruits
A bunch of ivy from beyond the river bend
The sweet scent strong the entire commute
My initial intentions only ever to play pretend

My own bottled nectar I sought to crave
It was lightning in a bottle I was looking to craft
Something to live far beyond the grave
Rolling up my sleeves and ready to graft

Luckily, I learnt early on of no guarantees
With perfection in mind, I was put to practice
Allowing those who wished to watch, but all they had to see
Was a Young Sick Bacchus

Many moons will soon fall behind the veil
Recognising that recognition may appear at a later time
I do not care - like a sailor, ready to set sail
Voyaging forward towards an even finer wine

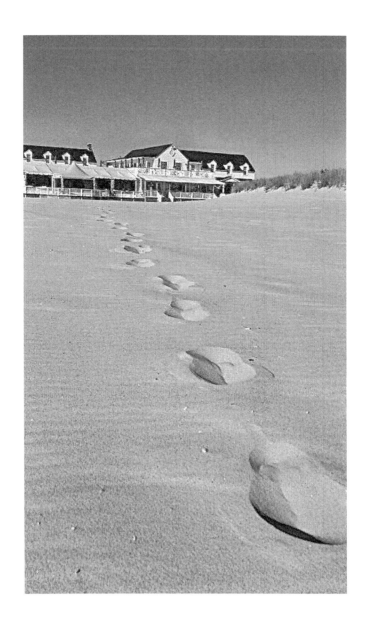

3

the sea

FOOTPRINTS IN THE SAND

I want to prove
That I was here
That I made an impact
And had something to say
Something to live for
And something worth dying for
That my time was truly spent
Every penny of my energy
Exchanged
On memories, achievements and
Accolades
That I learnt to better myself
Leaving a small mark
On a big world
Made valuable change
That I made those around me
Feel something
Whether a snigger or a laugh
I want to prove
That I was here
That I left some footprints
In the sand
And not to waste this
Incredible opportunity
That I have been gifted
Called life
So many people don't live
To their full potential
But that is their choice to make
I want to make sure
That when I am dead
And gone
My legacy

Will live on and long
Whether I am
Considered
A genius
A jack of all trades
Or
A master of one
Or maybe even none
I am
Indifferently idyllic
As long as I know
I tried
To live the best life
I could
That I walked every corner
Of this land
That when I was told to sit
I would stand
That I gave to many
A helping hand
But most importantly
I left
Footprints
in the sand

COLOURS

I am yellow and I am blue
I am every shade and every hue
Navy, baby, electric, and even royal too
I am every crashing wave colliding,
Every shade of the vastly deep sea
Can't you see?
I am every individual grain of sand,
From the darkest orange to the lightest yellow
I am each moment of the sunset spilling over the land
I am every time of day that the sun is bright
Yet, I am the darkest corner of the blackest night
Could that even be right?
I am as deep green as the densest forest,
Lighter tones of a lime as mellow
As emerald as the nation's meadow
Because I am yellow and I am blue
I am every shade and every hue
We are more than what we are painted to be
There are more colours beneath that of which the eye can see
Look closer

MELTING POT

Cold concrete walls
Warm in some places
But only for a few fleeting seconds
Where they had just been touched
Moulding like melted candle
Wax drips.
My eyes beaming red
Faded lasers trying to pierce
The squared walls
Moving towards the floor
Weakening in strength
Sourced internally from the core
The heat of my body burning
Misshapen and not yet finished
Melting
Fanning the flames and converting my vessel
To something unknown
The lasso is tightening
Closing in
And gone
Something even stronger
Cooking
Ready to be reborn

MAKING WAVES
(HAIKU)

Ready to rock the boat
Making waves when needed most
Be the change we need

ATLANTIS ADJACENT

Right when I least expect - it happens
As the last few drops of my coffee pour, right after I've collected
the post from the foot of the door
I find myself lost in the lost city, built on the foundations of the
opportunity cost
Spent, by previous choices I, myself have made

I roam free through the streets made up in my mind
Wandering through the kingdom that never came
Yearning for a life that does not exist
I grieve, because maybe, I just may not have let it

In the rare moments I am now alone
I am accompanied by the greener grass on the other side
And for just a moment, I lay in it and cry
Contemplating the alternative route, I should have taken through
life deep down inside

And as I grab the post, and take a sip of my coffee
I allow myself to wander for just a moment in time
To an alternative universe that had potential to survive
And I remind myself, that everything is fine

For the rest of my days, I will live Atlantis adjacent
Reflecting on the life beyond the fence that stretches outside my
window
Because nothing will ever be truly good enough
Yet I can't afford to be too complacent

LOST AT SEA

Winds of solid rock, at gale
Blustering seas, anchored
Kept down by hail

Submerged, steering south
The surface sprints further north
For success exists a ravishing drouth

Remaining breaths numbered
Three, two... I count
Refusing to fail, I fight the slumber

Losing sight of what lies above
My vision grows shrouded
Aquatics overhead act as flying doves

Suffocating on the inhaled pressure
Being swallowed alive in the midst
Finding hints of pleasure from the hidden treasure

Seeking growth within the challenge
From the depths of the darkest seas,
I scavenge

Do not sound the sirens when I am lost at sea
I need not be saved nor rescued
I am where I have to be

MEETING A MERMAID

When I was just a kid,
I always knew that mermaids exist
Even in my adolescence, I was sure
Beneath the surface society had created
They were kept at bay
Far away, from what was deemed as normal
Afraid, if given the chance,
At what they might say

Regardless, I remained adamant
I was certain
These creatures could exist
I knew that they were real
Living within an underworld
Beyond the fairytales we were told
On this planet which we shared
This unapologetic creature roamed

You see,
I wanted to swim like a mermaid
To tackle the currents with confidence,
With a passion and a flair
Live the life that I was supposed to live
Immersing myself in a new world unknown
One I didn't know where, but I knew
I belong

And when the moment finally came,
Once upon a time,
To discover that mermaids actually exist
I managed to hold it together, I insist.
I simply watched from afar in awe
From the coast, I watched them effortlessly swim
Confirming my suspicions,
Slowly, dipping my own toe in.

Knowing, that they were real
Is all that it truly took
To get me into the water waist-high
Alas, it didn't come to me over night.
There were skills that I had to learn and train
Which came to me over time
Because to strengthen my new backbone
I had to break a rotting spine

And now, I swim like a mermaid
I tackle the currents with confidence
With a passion and a flair
I am now unafraid of the unknown
Day by day, I assess the seas in which I swim
Gauging, if I'll feel unwelcome and ignored
Or be celebrated and adored

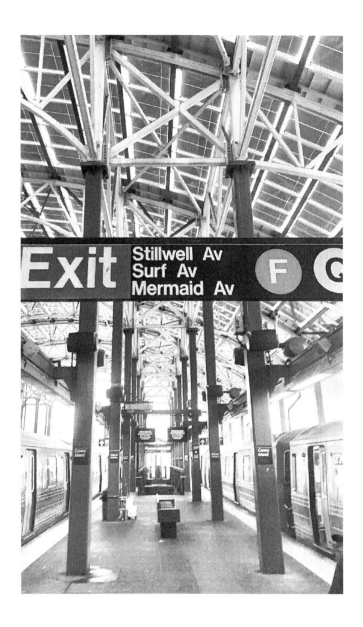

186

RIVER

The seeds I've sowed have sown
The fields I've tended to are grown
Sunflowers singing towards the sun
The wildflowers are matured, and it feels
As though my work here is truly done
And now,
After all is said and done
They shall whither
And at that point I know
I will call out for you
My River
To flourish the world that I have known
To stream down from the mountains
I have won
And take me away with you
Overboard and overcome
Washing away the world that I have known
Bringing me to new destinations
I could never have found alone
Pool by pool, they form a river
To flourish a new and greater land
A level playing field with greater crops to fuel
More seeds to sow, and work to do
My River
I will call out for you
Take me away
River won't you run to me
Oh River,
Won't you come to me

CHANGE

The world is changing
And so are we
A place demanding
Of more inclusivity
Still, I wonder
Why people are so enraged
At the simple idea of
Change
That is keeping our world clean
Repairing the damage done
For the future
Of our earth and sea
For our next of kin
Those we know
And them
We may never get to see
A world
Where including others
Is occurring
With welcoming arms
And if I may say,
Just because
You don't understand it
Just because you cannot see it
Hear it
Breathe it
Experience it
Does not mean
It is not
Real
Or valid
Our culture is based
On relatability
What makes us
Laugh
Cheer
And cry

But when it is not
Relatable
Those issues
Are pushed to the side
My simple ask
Is please
Do not resist.
Accept
Embrace
And love
Change
For a home
Where everyone
Feels welcome
Accepted and safe
In themselves
And the planet
And a society
That we can
Look on
In our graves
With relief
And think
Our kids
Will be
Okay.

BEACH BOY

As darkness folded, and the light awakened
He arose that dawn
Another day of adventure to spend
Under the world's eye
Subject to interpretation of others, at odds with his own will

He past the sundial atop the clocktower
Casting it's ever-moving shadow, in constant shift
Finding residence, he lay atop the sand
Overlooking the earth's edge
On the front line facing out towards the unknown

Many onlooker's past, going about their day
On their own journeys along the coastline
of chatter, gossip, silence and even retrospective thought
With a quick and passing glance, their opinions cast
In a fleeting moment, none were dignified, yet all held true

To some, to all, to one, to none,
He was as mellow as the sand was still
With the same potential aggression of the crashing waves across
the coastline
Considered waste, like the washed-up bottles on the shore
And as weak as the lacking heat from the sun's unimpressive
beam

Indifferent to the silent judgements emitted
Going about his day as originally planned
Subject to opinion, he lay in his subjectiveness
Because from the sun to the moon, the sea to the stars,
From dusk to dawn, his day was irreversibly idyllic

He understood the fluidity of one's perspective
Never fixed, like the shadow of the ever-moving sundial.
That the world we live in was painted,
With the blurred lines of water lilies
And the magic we have been granted to alter our own mindsets

Because to the scarce, the few, but more importantly himself,
He was as calm as the sand was still
As determined as the waves crashing across the coastline
Hopeful, like the washed-up message that lay hidden within the
bottle, if one had cared to notice
And as bright as the blinding light that came from the sun's
ever-impressive beam

Because no matter how far as the eye can see
Is never quite enough to see the detail that lies on the other side
As vast as the multitude of moods felt in a single day
Beauty lies in the eye of the beholder's perception
Fear residing within the eyes of the narrow-minded

With that, he found warmth in the hug of a chilling sea-breeze
Seeks comfort swimming above the depths of the darkest seas
Kindness in the actions of judgmental strangers
The duality of man is questioned, if not multiplied
As we stand, on the fine line of perspective and perception

Where the water meets the land
He is the waves, the ocean, the wind,
He is every grain of sand that collectively creates the coast
He is the sun, the heat and the light, the first sign of the shore's
twilight
He is each and every component that makes up the beach

The captain of his own soul
He vowed to constantly broaden his horizons
Seeking answers in other's intent, then solely in their actions, to
try to understand
And as the shadow of the sundial dwindled at dusk
He slowly began to sink into the sand

GAME OVER

Trying to capture that lightning in a bottle
A moment for life
I'm chasing in full throttle
There's a lot to learn from a game of roulette
And I haven't been striked out just yet

Many find comfort in the levels well-lived
Solace in the familiar streets walked
But I know I got much more game to play
I'm determined to level myself up, no cap
Ready to journey beyond the pre-planned map

The second you get complacent it's game over
No more wishes granted
All outta luck from the four-leaf clover
The unsung hero takes an unknowing knee
Three for three from the wishing tree

There's so much more beyond that little town
You gotta play it hard
Go for gold, grab your rightful crown
You're made for something much bigger
They swim in ponds, but you're the river

4

the stars

INVASIVE WALL FLOWERS

The vines fall tangled towards the ground,
slowly stringing along
Pouring over the painted pot from their roots
a beautiful song
Their melodies strung,
they harmonise together to a halting bridge
Quilting the gaps that could simply just be left
a song unsung
With no intentions
to cause such alluring havoc and disarray
These imprisoned wall flowers
can have so much more than expected to say

TROPHY

Hang me on your highest wall
Polish me like solid gold
Hold me to your highest regard
Your greatest glory never sold

Tell them of your admiration
Of your greatest achievement to date
A suited home would be pride of place
It wasn't destiny nor fate

Place me on your mantel
At the top of the crowded shelf
Shine a godly light upon me
That you wouldn't even believe yourself

Imprison me in a bel jar
For safety, to help ease the mind
Never let my colour fade
Or let my powerful shine go blind

Because I want to be your greatest feat
I just want to make you proud
Look towards the future with delight
A burst of gold to battle away the cloud

COWABUNGA

The 4th of July
The land of the free is sparkling
Written in fire across the sky
A nation blazing from the Atlantic
To Malibu and back
Taking orders and swerving corners
Supervising sodas and salted snacks
Sneaking shots in even creakier cabanas
Fleeing from the grip of the prison guards
Not yet loose after 2 to 3 bottled beers
And yet I am front and centre still
I've got the best seat in the house
Watching the movie from inside the silver screen
Cowabunga baby!
The reflections of multicoloured lights
Surfing the black waves
Although fixed to my assigned position
Intuitive timing and assumptions of limited intelligence
Makes for somewhat exquisite escapes
Sharing flashes of over-glorified glee
Joint efforts to catch ourselves during a mutual flee
Even then, as much as I hate to admit,
I couldn't feel more free

BEYOND THE BOARDROOM

There is a life that exists
Beyond the boardroom
Where you don't get sucked in and swept up
That is plentiful, fruitful and rich
To leave work at work is a promising deal
For a life that is real, with limited risk
Because beyond the boardroom
Is a world of complete enrichment
A place to accomplish your dreams
Where you prioritise your own fulfilment
And your soul blazingly gleams

THE REBEL ROLE MODEL

Struck like a lightning bolt
Oddly fitting like a glove
Cannot be defeated or defined
Of admiration, we end up following with love

A rebel with a cause
The unlikely selection by common jury
The reddest berry, cherry-picked of the bunch
Overflowing with benevolent fury

A contagious connection tough to construe
To the status quo, a leader of anarchy
Expanding mindful horizons
Through unbeatable and unwavering energy

An inspiration that just feels right
Striding the path less followed in a confident fashion
Through this rebel role model, we regularly gain
These outpouring waves of pure and potent passion

YOUNG HOLLYWOOD

Shots of sake off Hollywood and Highland
The lights of the city below, glittering like diamonds
I've killed the reality I once knew to be true
Living in a dream that I had once dreamt
Drinks filled with liquors we've never heard of
With strangers who aren't our friends
Nothing lasts forever
Except for tonight in my mind
We cheers to the dreamland
We've made of our lives
Tell the driver to take the long way
Through Mulholland for the view
Play that song that we once knew
That sang of a life like this
It went something along the lines of do-do-da-do
I've finally put myself first
I came as I am
And tomorrow I'm leaving a better man
Hungover and a little dehydrated
I am happy.
How many people can truly say that for themselves?
I've found the entrance to the secret garden
And the gate is somewhere between Sunset and Santa Monica
Nestled between the bosom of boujee hotels and strip clubs
High up in the hills,
We pour another drink and cheers to nothing
We are privileged, but we are grateful
Hoping tomorrow will never come
We get messily graceful
And for tonight,
We are young Hollywood

MTV RAISED ME

I grew up an infant, in front of the box
Eager eyes, watching on
Pool parties of empty pools
With people performing their catchy rock songs
And then it evolved.
I became engrossed in the houses that they held
Plaques and trophies proudly displayed upon the walls
Lines of cars appropriately placed
I didn't want to settle for anything less
I wanna do it all, I would think to myself.
I became obsessed
Not with a life of over excess
But with the idea that anything is possible
That if I can put my mind to it
I can make my own dreams come true
I can be like them. Me.
I can be the M in MTV.
I held zero interest in being from a small country
And an even smaller town.
I believed in a bigger world that was made for me
That was full of endless possibilities,
And that I, myself, was credible
Of all potential capabilities.

NORTH STAR

(HAIKU)

The North Star calls out
My next adventure awaits
Beyond the window

SUNDOWN

As golden hour begins to rust
The sky finally folding in on us
We'll lay on the grass to let our eyes adjust
And with twilight's chill creeping in my bones
Now as our day is coming to a close

I'll be with you at sundown

Shortly we'll watch the daylight turn to dark
The silhouette of the city's shadow stark
Reflecting on the day that's done
The endless laughs, the priceless fun
For now, and forever I'll hold you close
At each and every sundown

And when sundown finally strikes
Alone on the grass
My knees held tightly in my arms
Looking out upon the fading view
Questioning the way the world works
I'll think of you

I AM GOD

Of my ideas
I created a world
Of love and loss
Hope and despair
Hurdling it up into the air
Still, it sat amongst the stars
A moon
Lighting the night
And from afar it looked small
Insignificant
And like anything else
Passable
But if you looked closer
You would really see
Something bigger
Of perpetuity.
Beaming
Existing
And real
A manifestation
The fruit of my labour
Ripe and ready
For digestion
Observed and examined
Each idea
A bluebottle
Buzzing around
My cluttered mind
Opening the window
Clearing the noise
Setting them free
A representation
Purely
Of me

OVERRIPE

All of a sudden, life is moving at a rapid pace
On the conveyer belt left with little to no space
The next lobster in line just waiting to be plucked
I want to bite the hand, and tell it to get fucked

I wanna pause this show and take a well-earned break
Make a cup of tea before any more mistakes
The idea of Oblivion at times, doesn't sound so bad
To hear the sweet nothings of the silence - I demand!

Move to a secluded cabin in which I can hide
No one can find the woodlands address I choose to reside
Alleviate the narrowing pressures of this war
Maybe, I don't want to be a diamond anymore

For now, I shall simply step back before I go berserk
And be left to lie in some forgotten works
Overripe and feeling so worn out
I would hate to ever have to swim with the trout

5

the dusk

QUARANTINE

(MARCH 2020)

Fantasia's playing on the television
The colours the most vibrant I've seen all day
The violins from 1940 still thrillingly played
Probably a level louder than they should be
The sims deluxe is downloading
As the paints on our self-portraits dry
The sadness and fear in my face
Are at war on the canvas
With the golden glimmer of hope
I'm secretly hiding inside
These days don't feel much like living
As we live through this moment of
World history
Letting some of my planned life goals go
Trying to take back control of what we can
Stimulating our senses with past pastimes
New consoles and even some games
Older than ourselves
Tomorrow, *Future Nostalgia* is released
And I couldn't find a title more fitting
For this time in which we are living
The umpteenth Groundhog Day
Holding my breath that it stays this way
In a sense
My only goal to make it out alive
With those who I entered with,
Making it safely out the other side

MORNING'S CALL
(HAIKU)

It's sad to ponder
The beauty of morning's call
Is not seen by all

KUMBAYA

Beyond the hilltop meadow,
sat a man, sitting alone by his campfire
The other side of the hill
'Kumbaya', he sang along
By his lonesome, he was going strong
'Come by here', he called out in a desperation so dire
In search of still waters,
He was a man trying to take control of fire

Quietly chanting Kumbaya, he yearned
By the third verse of his fourteenth attempt,
He was eventually joined by another,
Who strolled into his inner circle with supreme serenity
Silently, they took a seat beside the man
In the company of, the embodiment of peace he now was.
Whom of which he kindly asked for their advice
In learning how to take control of his fire

All this time,
He was able to sustain a manageable campfire,
keeping the flames alight yet tame
A game of backgammon, back and forth they fought
Beside him they spoke, a confident speech so eloquently soft.
In which they said;
'Keep singing your song
Don't sing for others, but only for an audience of yourself
Don't seek the validation of others, of which you cannot keep
It cannot be bottled,
like the fire in which you reap.
Instead, let the voices speak
Contradictions in life are essential to exist
For every judgement made, we are to obtain five ourselves
We must understand the complexity of human nature
And that in itself, can be hard to do
But to take control of fire,
You are capable to fan the flames of which you speak

You must learn to live your life as only you wish
Not the life decided for you, by the company
You may or may not keep'

The man was startled,
but not because he had learnt something new
But because he had been told something
of which he always knew to be true.
And so, he sat beyond the hilltop meadow,
Alone by his campfire
With still waters in sight,
A man who was learning how to take control of fire

SUGAR COATED KISS

You call me handsome
I call you unsure
Settling it like adults
You tell me
'You're very mature'

As we kiss goodbye
Back to our own separate lives
'We'll be in touch'
We say to each other
We both know deep down
Never to end up seeing one another

So, we put it to bed
And we kiss this goodnight
It was short while it lasted
Nevertheless, an utter delight
Leaving the scene of the unsolved crime
With nothing but unresolved doubt in my mind

You and your antics I'll miss no doubt
As we decide to part ways
With a sugar-coated kiss
'I'm sad', I desperately confess
One last kiss
None the less

COWBOYS AND INFLUENCERS

The old wild west for a new age
The internet it's battlefield,
As they go to war
All trying to outdo the other more

The world we knew has changed
One step forward, two steps back
It's a given that history will repeat itself
With everyone only in it for themselves

Nowadays, the cowboys and influencers are rife
In a fight to the death, for followers and likes
We try to distinguish the difference between the two
This newfound culture, hoping to bid adieu

Because they're trying to coax us
Into living a dream of a reality, that just isn't true
Fooling us into buying the next big thing
We must free ourselves from the lasso of this rodeo ring

The old wild west for a new age
The internet it's battlefield,
As they go to war
How much longer do we have to watch this for?

27 CLUB

Sitting in eternal isolation
Gives you time to reflect
On the 27 years past
And the ones I hope to have left
Reaching this stage of life
Is a reward in itself.
The accomplishments I've made
Sit pride of place on the shelf
As I come up to the dreaded crossroads
Between what is considered young and old
Having to make life or death decisions
On whether to check or fold
I welcome the change with open arms
As I approach the entrance to the 27 club
Plucking the next of my roses
From life's nettle-filled shrub

I STILL MISS THE DAYS WHEN IT RAINS IN LA

I still miss the days when it rains in LA
Driving through the city and I'm singing in the rain,
This place loved for the sun, a permanent holiday,
Here I am in the mi(d)st, feeling this type of way,
the rain comes crashing down a storm
When it rains here, it pours, and I finally
Understand the validity of that statement now
Can I keep you, to the sky I ask aloud
Do you want to keep me too?
Pedestrians laugh as we pass
Men and their dogs,
Iced coffees in hand
We'll meet on the corner of Hollywood and Vine every time,
pick me up from the bus station
Holding me in your arms each time
Through the canyons, we'll cruise
All the way down Ventura just like the old days?
Losing myself in the music of the city,
I walk with a soundtrack to my steps
not able to see the wood from the palm.
We broke up but I still feel like there's a chance,
because I still miss the days even when it rains in LA,
it makes me feel like I belong,
because nothing is always perfect,
every moment of any day.
How the streets would turn to sunken streams
And highway rivers run through the city strong
Let me meet your demands,
I don't want much or to use you for what you have,
I just want you.

It wasn't supposed to always be this way,
but here I am,
and I still miss the days when it rains in LA,
Because you're just a dream some of us had
But with all the hopes and dreams
and the promises we made
Down the drain they all got washed away,
the sins we had, you and I, LA
I'll keep them close, in the hopes
That we meet again someday
Until then, I'll reminisce on the days it rained
Because it was in those moments, I knew
My companionship to you was forever claimed

MY DEAR FRIEND

My dear friend
Comes to me at the most unexpected times
On the darkest of nights, I hear the door knocking
A breaking and entry of kinds

Although not always welcome, he confidently arrives
To disturb the night which I had planned
Making himself more than at home
Bringing with him, melancholic memories at hand

I am somewhat guilty in enjoying his presence
Letting him have his say
Allowing him to swallow the atmosphere of the room
His presence is notable, and here to stay

In the midst of the melodrama
He reminds me of the times past
How much life has changed, and what could have been
From reality now, a stark contrast

Despite the despair he has brought
I allow myself in the moment to wallow - just for today
Eventually, he will come to go, and I know for sure,
Tomorrow will be a better day

DAISY

Strolling through the meadow
We were often led astray
But then you gave me a daisy
And together we made a chain
With every day that followed
Feeling like an endless summer
We were dancing in the rain

FINDING MY FOREVER HOME

When my body and soul have finally come to end their
courtship, and I am on the lookout for my forever home

Allow me to set up camp along the Isle of Doagh
Watching over my homeland from its most northerly point
How noble
Where I will watch the ones, I've come to know
And those I've come to love and cherish
Live on and long
Within a respectfully peaceful distance I will remain
In tow

It goes without saying that a piece of me will always be present
Either in person or in spirit
Or even perhaps
In a perfectly polished ornament
In the north facing room sitting above the double sized
windowsill
That rarely saw nothing but shadows constantly in search for the
sun
Somewhere where time was well spent dreaming of a land
Where I would call my forever home

If I had to pick between a local hidden pier or a popular
promenade
My response would be, "maybe both"
A reflection of how my life was lived
Never wanting to settle on any one given thing
Always striving for more
For every cycle on the unwinding country roads down to the
pier
To bask in a few moments of hidden heaven were filled with joy
As those spent walking, running and swimming alongside the
infamous Blackrock

But how could I possibly not find a home along Franklin
Avenue
The silver lining where the lived-in streets and the land of
endless possibilities met
Where tears were a relief and the laugher were so hard it was
sore
Where luck was imminent, and I grabbed every opportunity with
full steam vigor
Squeezing every last little piece of chance that I could grasp
Before my time was inevitable to come to a close
Residing in this place where I felt more freedom than I ever
possibly could have known

And when my body and soul have finally come to end their
courtship, and I am on the lookout for my forever home

Cast me like a net along the Atlantic Ocean
So I can capture within it the secrets of the world which lies
beneath
The ocean becoming my final form of divine being
Because if you can't beat 'em, join 'em,
And I intend to.
Skimming the seas from coast to coast, where so much of my
heritage lies
I will finally allow the power of the sea to succumb me
Allowing me to finally face the fears I once frantically dread

Or perhaps, perch me within the gardens of Fernhill,
High up in the Dublin mountains
The tranquil bliss in this place where we had the chance to reside
Together, it was here we found our harmonious place to hide
Each evening as the leaves of the trees danced across the carpet,
shortly after six,
A place so peaceful that we couldn't even hear the turbulent
traffic of the cars pass

Scatter me among the leaves and I will dance forever as my final
oath
Overlooking the south side of the city, and all along the way to
Howth

And when my body and soul have finally come to end their
courtship, I will have found the many habitats in which I shall
call home...

Particularly a strong contender along the Pacific Coast Highway
Where the Santa Monica mountains meet
The stretched shorelines of the beach
Not having to make a choice of which of those I prefer, as
people to tirelessly ask
But settling on a resting place that simply encompasses all of the
above where I may bask
So, lay me to rest smack bang right in the middle of Malibu
Because whether you are to decide which is more relevant;
imaginary or true
This is where I have been living my whole life
The entire time with you

MULHOLLAND DRIVE

At the after-party in the Hollywood Hills
You helped me forget about all my cheap thrills
Bringing me into your world
And a very different kind of life

Soft-top black BMW, roof down
Taking me for a ride
It was in each other we found our fun
In me, you found a boy on the run

Hopeful for a Hollywood-like ending on the big screen
I learnt my lines, eagerly acting out my scenes
Because Norma Jean was just like me
Before she became a Monroe

But you had your dark side
And you wanted to hide
You told me I was your first and only man
For the longest time

Things soon came to a hesitant halt - as they often have
A car crash happening in slow motion
The damage done to a broken heart
From the wreck, we were torn apart

Now I'm back in my homeland, in another world
And you're still living it up, deep down in the underworld
At times, I wonder if you still think about me;
How the future was supposed to be

It'll be just like in the movies
We'll pretend to be someone else
Cause in the moments captured, my fantasies came true
And forevermore a fantasy - will just have to do

6

the dawn

YOUR WORLD, MY WORLD

I occupied my days in scenes of blue
In search of skies, similar too
Often filled with melancholic moments
That was the old me, but you

Swam through life in a sea of red
Rose-tinted glasses, with opposite intent
A burning building of flaming frustrations
No signs of fanning out, and then

Lanes merged, a sudden crash
Forming a new and unexpected lilac path
We were found, skipping through purple rain
Living in lavish lavender, just like that

Nothing was ever the same
Previous problems overcame, no one to blame
Your world became a thrilling track which took wings
Your song now sung over silver strings, and I

Found something greater than expected
I became an awarded miner, of life's great expedition
Mine to own, a prize to behold until I am old
My world became gilded, in solid gold

WAKING UP ON CLOUD 9

The morning has come around as promised, once again
Delayed moments my eyes spend
to fully awaken from the blinding strain
But this time I have awoken,
Far away from where I used to consider home
Somewhere in Dreamland,
I could have only ever imagined to have known

Testing the strength of my senses, I explore
and examine every little detail
Trying to understand my current surroundings a bit more
Within this celestial abode,
I feel further and further away from the ground
The morning alarm breaks the silence
Startling me as the trumpets sound

In the ways of an eager historian, I am curious
Eager to explore my most recent subject
Secretly, hoping for a result not spurious
I search for clues to understand
Brow raised, and suspicious to find
Anything that I can hold onto
With my findings safely enshrined

What did I ever do to end up here?
What have I done to deserve this hand of cards?
Is heaven as heavenly as this moment appears?
The alarm repeats once more
Reminiscent of a Main Street Disneyland parade
It brings me back to reality
My happiness from this particular morning yet to fade

A breakfast follows, fit for two kings
Tasting menus to satisfy all curiosity
The dawn of the morning springs
We sling ourselves across the comforter
Back-to-back daytime TV on a roll
We sink further into the clouds
I grab another bowl

I take a break to walk atop the clouds
Taking in the magnificent views
Here above the noise and the crowds
Admiring the fallen houses upon the hill
Perched in their place of residence, they're stuck
I see my reflection in their windows
Elevated, and can't believe my luck

Because I wake up here, and you're there
Looking you in your eyes
You run your fingers through my hair
Tossing and turning until noon
Mornings like this are what makes life taste so divine
There's a certain richness to the flavour
Waking up on cloud nine

MY LIFE AS AN ACTOR

Life can be sweet
In Paradise Cove
This world that I've created
And this story that I've told

This tale is one for the ages
These parts that I've been playing
In this, my greatest role yet
Not much preparation for it do we get

As I awake every morning
Like a seasoned professional, I learn my lines
Preparing for this acting role
Not many can read between the lines

This land of make believe
Where we are all playing a part
A role to be filled, an actor billed
Standing ovation for a performance off the charts

The job requirements are never ending
I've played many roles in my day
A child, a student, a mentor, a teacher
Versatile talent, if I so may say

'Fake it 'til you make it'
You have heard those before, you preach
At times I want to leave this dead-end job
Head stage left, and right to the blissful beach

HALL OF MIRRORS

Take a walk through the hall of mirrors
And tell me what you see
Objects in the reflection may be distorted upon view

A long, lonely stride for any straggler
Walking further from reality, once inside
Many an adventurer have withdrew

Presented with yourself in many forms
People who pass must find their inner strength
Their character, on the firing line for review

The hall of mirrors holds a kaleidoscope of colour
Often an opportunity to see yourself in new light
Here, you see every shade, and every hue

The reflections of yourself can be at-times unsightly
Misshapen, with a twisted representation
More likely misaligned, from what you thought you knew

In the hall of mirrors, there is no single reflection
That is accurately and wholeheartedly true, however
All of it is you

MONKEY SEE, MONKEY DO

There's nothing more powerful
Than to show them how it's done
Swinging tree to tree,
The outcome is second to none
Gripping the vines tight
Is just one part of all the fun
Diving in the deep end
And swimming towards the sun
So lead by example,
And continue to make leaps
While jumping through the jungle
Proving the possibilities of landing atop mountain steeps
Fear not, and don't fret if they don't immediately follow
Just make sure to stay consistent with your run
And as time goes by,
Eventually, they may very well may come.

TRAIN OF THOUGHT
(HAIKU)

On the tracks of life
The train of thought never stops
But can be controlled

COMMON GROUND

When you created a glass ceiling,
I started to build myself a stair of solid stone
To rise above and carry on,
Stepping on every misconstrued underestimation,
Each acting as a powerful steppingstone

Alas, let us find common ground
Atop the glass ceiling that I have now shattered
From your failed attempts of stopping me in my tracks.
I shall not be pigeonholed or have my capabilities capped
Free to achieve what I believe I can

Here, I stand in a line with those alike,
Forming a chain of an unbreakable bond
Together, we sing in a choir
In perfect harmony upon our newly crowned stage
We continue to rise, we levitate, we fly

There are no grounds for prejudice, or unjust hate
Still, we welcome you to join us if you will,
And you should -
This place of serenity is nothing like anything else around,
And the potential here, is truly renowned

AFTER LIFE

For a moment,
I had it all figured out
I thought I knew what I wanted in life.
Meeting with friends at weekends,
We would discuss the plans we had all pre-planned
Blueprints, to our seemingly short-lived lives
Focusing on what we wanted the most
And for me, it was simple…
Fancy clothes and shinier shoes
Manors surrounded with perpetual land
A growing reputation of power to mount
The steadily expanding income of an even healthier bank account.
An aspirational bunch, sharing our shared objectives over brunch,
We would discuss in detail what we sought out of this life.

It wasn't until later that evening, when a storm finally came
Lightning struck, and it hit a nerve
No longer seeing the light, in what I believed to be right
I realised that I never considered what I sought - in the *afterlife*.
I struggled to ponder,
What would be my lasting impression?
What was my contribution to the world?
How will I be remembered when I'm gone?
These were all questions, I failed to comprehend
So, I thought.
And when the storm had finally came and went,
Something significant happened to me that night
Because it was in that moment, I decided
that I would write.

CHARACTER

Who are you?
Have you made a conscious decision deep down inside?
To objectify our individual character goals
At one stage or several, I believe that we have all tried

We must understand if character is really chosen
If it is something for us to truly decide
Whether we as people browse a catalogue
Picking a suited personality to live out with pride

In reality, it is with every brick we form,
Cemented together, the perfect storm
Stitched piece by piece through the act of living
Is when true character is actually born.

Because in our very own stories, we are the lead
It is in every other book in which we feature
We must be conscious of how our character is interpreted
As a knight in shining armour, or a great-winged evil creature

When it comes to the perspective of other protagonists
In the library of storybooks, we play many a role
Nothing to fear but simple misunderstandings
Knowing who we really are, deep down in our souls

It is the content of our character
We have the power to control each day
Alas, on how it is understood
We are not the ones, who have the final say

The ease of accepting misconceptions is more often rare
It is one of life's hardest lessons to learn not to care
The collision of opinion on our character
Will always hold a constant home up in the air

So, who are you?
Is it really ever for us to actually decide?
When it comes to how others will tell tales of us
With perspectives, the only power we have is to guide.

LIBERTY AT LAST

Heavy are the chains I've held in my fists
Dragging along by my weakened wrists
Weighted down by ton weight of thought
Shackled to the ground
By the depths of public perception

Looking on in admiration of those who run free
Whipped by chains at every bend
Tackled by sour scourges of judgement
Poisoned by preconceived notions of character
Continue on their journey through the straight and narrow

Yet, here I am, held captive and trapped
In this pigeon-hole mindset presented by others
A great misunderstanding of our minds potential
And as we grow older,
I feel the prison grow smaller and smaller

As some seek comfort in the darkened box,
I see a crack of light, a shimmer of hope
Illuminating the small space, I have found myself succumb to.
The key: my freedom of expression and thought
Freedom to challenge what we have been presented with
Freedom to even just try –
Freedom to learn, change, expand and fly

And now the golden ray has begun
To burn away slowly, at this shield of grey
Distracted by each and everything that I can finally see
Thoughts of summer flings that the sunshine brings
And the smells of sprouting daffodils and daisies
Slowly, begin to bring me back to life

Here, the waterfalls are flowing north
Trying to find a cloud to crash against, in place of rocks
Yet – there is no stopping them.
My perspective has shifted,
I am lifted
Now I am elevated and towering towards the sky.

This feeling may not last forever,
No fixed destination fit for a full circle finale
As in this game of life, it will likely come to pass
But for right now, I am free
And I can truly feel
Liberty
        at
            last.

NEW SKIN

Once upon a time…
       I hopped on a plane just once or twice
              Thought I could save me from myself
                     But I couldn't run, nowhere to hide

18 years young
       My own biggest threat
              I wanted to go home
                     But I hadn't found it yet

Desperate for any dream to wake
       I searched for answers in other's arms
              I didn't know what was to come
                     A decade strong of self-inflicted harm

As the season's past,
       The world was seen an unsightly plight
              This house was nobody's home
                     I saw the darkness in the Christmas lights

But I wanted to no longer live a life in fear of shame
       Deciding to no longer wait for a when
              Casting the papers of unwritten drafts aside
              I grabbed the pen

A boy bit by a lizard
       I felt my skin begin to shed
              Stepping out of an empty vessel
                   I saw an opening - and fled

Once upon a time…
       I dreamt of bearing what was beneath my skin
              And when I think of how things
                 have changed since then -
                   I grin

Printed in Great Britain
by Amazon

74960452R00156